...*nt Pictures*

Respiratory diseases

by

Peter J Barnes MA DM DSC FRCP
Professor of Thoracic Medicine, National Heart and Lung Institute,
and Consultant Physician, Royal Brompton Hospital, London, UK

Series Editor
J Richard Smith MD MRCOG
Senior Lecturer and Honorary Consultant Gynaecologist
Charing Cross and Westminster Medical School
Chelsea and Westminster Hospital, London, UK

Illustrated by
Dee McLean, MeDee Art, London, UK

HEALTH PRESS

Oxford

Patient Pictures – Respiratory Diseases
First published 1997
Reprinted 2003

© 1997 Health Press Limited
Elizabeth House, Queen Street, Abingdon, Oxford OX14 3JR

A CIP catalogue record for this title is available from the British Library.

ISBN 1-899541-40-3

The author wishes to thank Dr David Hansell, Department of Imaging,
Royal Brompton Hospital, for providing the X-rays and CT scans
that are reproduced in this book.

Typeset by Impressions Design & DTP, Bicester, UK
Printed by Quadrant, Hertford, UK

Contents

Reproduction authorization

The purchaser of this *Patient Pictures* series title is hereby authorized to reproduce, by photocopy only, any part of the pictorial and textual material contained in this work for non-profit, educational, or patient education use. Photocopying for these purposes only is welcomed and free from further permission requirements from the publisher and free from any fee.

The reproduction of any material from this publication outside the guidelines above is strictly prohibited without the permission in writing of the publisher and is subject to minimum charges laid down by the Publishers Licensing Society Limited or its nominees.

Signed *Sarah Redston* Publisher
Health Press Limited Oxford

The publisher and the authors have made every effort to ensure the accuracy of this book, but cannot accept responsibility for any errors or omissions.

Author's preface

Diseases of the lungs and airways are extremely common, and are a
frequent reason for referral and admission to hospital. A bewildering
variety of tests are now available for investigating lung diseases – some
of which can be performed in general practice, but most of which need
to be performed in hospital. Many lung diseases are, however, managed
in general practice, and asthma, which is now the commonest disease,
is often treated in this setting by specialist nurses.

This book is designed to help health professionals explain lung and
airway diseases and their treatment with the aid of simple pictures.
It also explains the various procedures that may be needed to diagnose
and treat these diseases. I hope that this book will provide useful
information and reassurance, so that patients will have a better
understanding of their disease and will be less anxious when attending
the hospital to see a specialist or undergo specific investigations.
I hope that the format used in this book may help the doctor and
health professional as well as the patient by providing useful and easily
communicated information.

Peter J Barnes MA DM DSc FRCP
Professor of Thoracic Medicine,
National Heart and Lung Institute,
and Consultant Physician,
Royal Brompton Hospital, London, UK

The chest and lungs

- The lungs are two air-filled organs located in the chest. They are separated from the abdomen by a flat muscle called the diaphragm.

- Each lung is covered by a pleural membrane. This membrane is separated from the chest wall by a film of liquid that lubricates the movements of the lungs.

- As the chest expands when a breath is taken, the lungs enlarge and air is drawn in through the airways.

- Air enters the nose and mouth, and passes through the 'voice box' (larynx) into the main windpipe (trachea). The trachea divides into two airways, each of which is called a bronchus. The airways branch like a tree, ending with very small airways deep in the lungs.

- Each airway is lined by cells which have fine hairs (cilia) that keep the airway clean. There is a layer of muscle under these cells that can contract and lead to narrowing of the airways under some circumstances.

- The smallest airways end in grape-like structures called alveoli. The alveoli have thin walls that are lined with fine blood vessels. This enables oxygen to pass into the blood and be carried around the body. Carbon dioxide also passes out of the blood so that it can be breathed out.

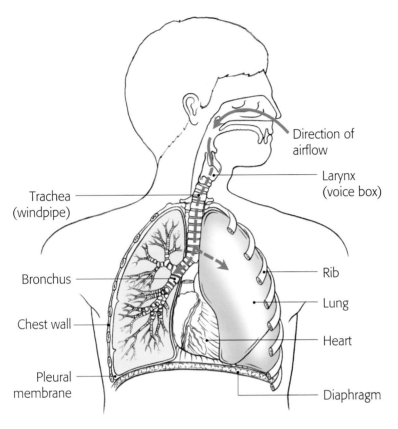

Direction of airflow

Larynx (voice box)

Trachea (windpipe)

Bronchus

Chest wall

Pleural membrane

Rib

Lung

Heart

Diaphragm

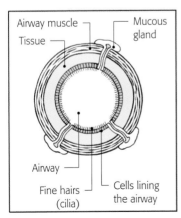

Airway muscle

Mucous gland

Tissue

Airway

Fine hairs (cilia)

Cells lining the airway

The airway is made up of several layers

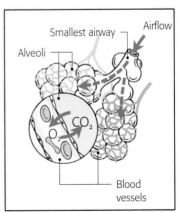

Smallest airway

Airflow

Alveoli

CO_2

O_2

Blood vessels

Gas exchange occurs in the alveoli

X-rays and other imaging investigations

- A chest X-ray is useful for looking at the lungs and airways. The lungs normally appear black on the chest X-ray, but in some diseases a 'shadow' may be seen. There are many causes of lung shadows and other investigations will be needed to discover what the problem is.

- A CT (computerized tomography) scan takes several X-ray pictures at different points throughout the chest, rather like slices through a loaf of bread. The CT scan gives a good idea of what is causing the shadow and exactly where it is in the chest. A CT scan involves lying still on a table in the scanner for up to 30 minutes. Although this is a bit claustrophobic, it is not painful.

- Occasionally, a ventilation–perfusion scan of the lungs is necessary, if clots on the lung (pulmonary embolism) are suspected. This involves an injection of a radioactive substance into a vein that enables the blood vessels of the lungs to be seen on the X-ray, and breathing in a radioactive gas so that the X-ray will show where the air goes when it is breathed in.

- The dose of X-rays used in all these tests is very small.

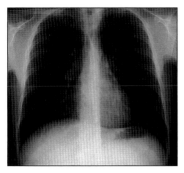

On a normal chest X-ray, the
lungs appear black

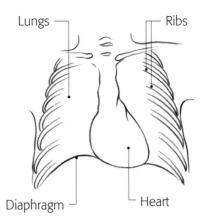

Lungs — Ribs

Diaphragm — Heart

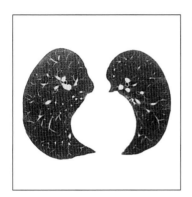

Normal CT scan section
through the lower lungs

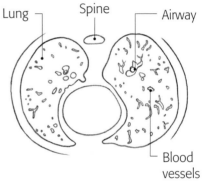

Lung — Spine — Airway

Blood
vessels

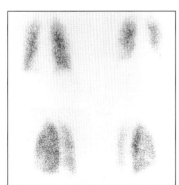

Ventilation scan of the lungs

The ventilation scan shows
which parts of the lungs are
ventilated when air is breathed
in. This normal scan shows air
is distributed to all areas

Peak flow measurements

- A peak flow meter records the maximum (peak) flow of air that can be breathed out. The peak flow measurement is a convenient measure of how much the airways are narrowed in asthma. It is also a good indicator of how well asthma is being controlled by treatment – the larger the peak flow measurement, the better the asthma is being controlled.

- Peak flow meters, which can be obtained on prescription, are often given to patients to use at home to monitor their treatment.

- Many patients are given a peak flow chart to record daily measurements. Peak flow is usually recorded first thing in the morning and last thing at night, before any inhaler is used. It is sometimes useful to repeat the measurement 15 minutes after using the blue (reliever) inhaler to see how much improvement is possible.

- A big difference between morning and evening values usually indicates poor control of asthma. You should know the best value that you have achieved and, by comparing this with your current measurement, you and your doctor will be able to tell how bad your asthma is and whether you need to increase the amount of treatment that you are taking.

PEAK FLOW METER

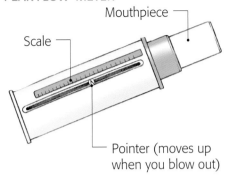

Mouthpiece

Scale

Pointer (moves up
when you blow out)

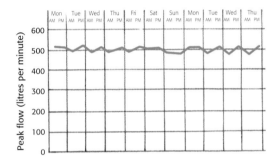

Peak flow of a
person without
asthma showing
normal values
throughout the day
with little variation
over the week

HOW TO RECORD PEAK FLOW

- Hold the meter horizontally in such a way as to avoid obstructing the movement of the pointer

- Take a deep breath in

- Put your lips around the mouthpiece then blow out as hard and fast as you can into the mouthpiece of the meter. It is not necessary to keep blowing out – a short sharp blow is what is needed

- Read the level of peak flow from the pointer position on the scale

- Three blows should be performed on each occasion with a short rest between each blow. Record only the highest of the three values

Spirometry

- Spirometry is the most widely used test to investigate lung disease. This test assesses how well the lungs can breathe using an instrument called a spirometer.

- Spirometry involves taking a full breath in and then blowing the air out as fast as possible until the lungs are empty. The amount of air breathed out over a period of time is recorded on a paper chart or electronically.

- Spirometry can help to diagnose all types of lung disease. It can distinguish between diseases that involve narrowing of the airways, such as asthma and chronic bronchitis, and diseases in which there is loss of lung capacity, such as lung fibrosis.

- Spirometry is also useful in asthma to measure the response to bronchodilator drugs given via the blue (reliever) inhaler. An initial measurement is made before the inhaler is used and another measurement is taken 15 minutes after inhaling two puffs. Patients with asthma can usually breathe out 15% more air after they have used their inhaler, depending on how well controlled their asthma is.

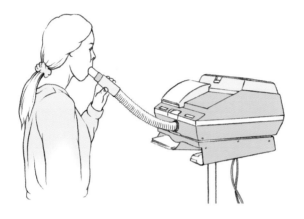

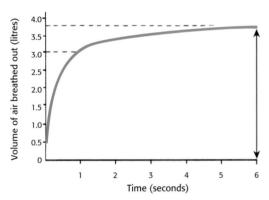

SPIROMETER TRACE

The total volume of air that can be breathed out is known as the vital capacity. This is a measure of the amount of useful lung volume. In normal people, over three-quarters of the vital capacity can be breathed out within 1 second

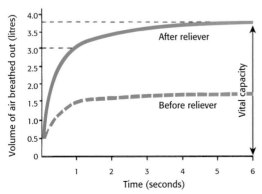

SPIROMETRY IN ASTHMA

Spirometry is useful to measure the response to treatment. After using a blue (reliever) inhaler, patients with asthma can breathe out more air, showing that the functioning of the lungs has improved

Other breathing tests

- In addition to spirometry, a number of other breathing tests are available to diagnose and assess lung diseases. The more complicated tests are usually performed in the Lung Function Laboratory in hospital.

- Gas transfer measurements show how efficiently inhaled air in the lungs enters the bloodstream. The test involves breathing in a small amount of a 'tracer' gas (carbon monoxide). Patients are then asked to breathe slowly into a device that analyses the gases breathed out. Gas transfer across the lungs is reduced in emphysema and lung fibrosis.

- The amount of oxygen and carbon dioxide entering the bloodstream may be measured in a blood sample if the lung disease is severe. This is used to assess whether extra oxygen needs to be given through a mask.

- Accurate recordings of the volume of the lungs may be made using a perspex 'body box'. The patient sits in an airtight box and breathes through a mouthpiece. The test usually takes 15–30 minutes and helps to diagnose certain types of lung disease, such as emphysema and lung fibrosis, in which the lung volume changes.

- Exercise testing involves measuring lung function and the levels of oxygen and carbon dioxide after exercising on a treadmill or on a fixed bicycle, which is like an exercise bike, while breathing into a monitoring device. This test is used when breathlessness on exercise is the major problem. It can help the doctor to decide whether this symptom is due to lung disease or heart disease.

RECORDING LUNG VOLUMES

You will be asked to:

*   sit in a box made of perspex and breathe gently through a mouthpiece

*   take a full breath in then breathe out

*   pant

EXERCISE TESTING

*   Your peak flow will be measured by spirometry before you start the exercise

*   You will then be asked to exercise on a treadmill (as shown) or on an exercise bicycle for 5–6 minutes

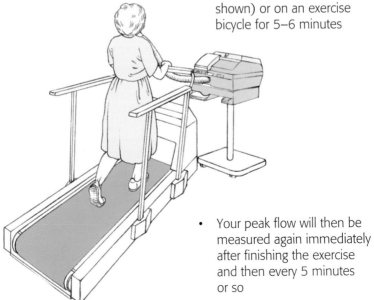

*   Your peak flow will then be measured again immediately after finishing the exercise and then every 5 minutes or so

Allergy and skin testing

- Skin prick tests are used to determine whether you have an allergy and what things you are allergic to.

- A drop of liquid containing a small amount of a substance known to cause allergy is placed on the forearm. A small sterilized needle is then pressed into the skin to break the surface. Several solutions are usually tested, including grass pollen, house dust, house dust mite, cat, dog and mould spores, together with a neutral solution and a histamine solution (histamine always gives a positive response to show that the test is working).

- A positive response appears within 15 minutes as a red area (flare) with a central raised section (weal) that is itchy. The size of the weal and flare indicate the degree of allergy to each substance tested.

- About one-third of people will have at least one positive reaction. Usually several tests are positive. Patients with hayfever will have a positive reaction to grass pollen, whereas asthmatic patients who have wheezing throughout the year often have a positive reaction to house dust mite.

- Skin tests can show whether asthma is due to an allergy. They may also indicate those things that are most likely to make the asthma worse.

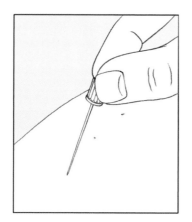

SKIN TESTING

A small drop containing allergy extract is pressed into the skin using a small sterilized needle

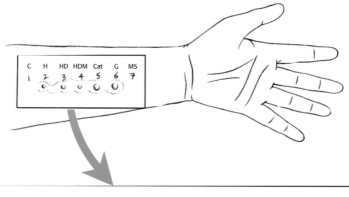

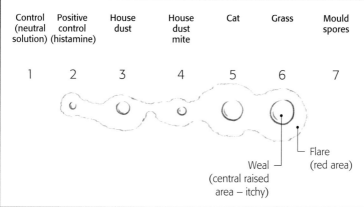

Control (neutral solution)	Positive control (histamine)	House dust	House dust mite	Cat	Grass	Mould spores
1	2	3	4	5	6	7

Weal (central raised area – itchy)

Flare (red area)

This test shows positive responses to house dust, house dust mite, cat and grass, and a negative response to mould spores

Bronchoscopy

- Bronchoscopy is an examination of the lungs using a flexible fibre-optic 'telescope' called a bronchoscope.

- The investigation is usually performed as a day-case procedure and takes about 1 hour. Occasionally, it may be necessary to stay in hospital if other tests are also to be carried out.

- Local anaesthetic is sprayed into the nose and the mouth to prevent discomfort and coughing during the procedure. A sedative and an injection to dry up the secretions in the airways may also be given. Patients with asthma or chronic bronchitis will often be given a nebulizer containing a drug before the procedure to prevent wheezing.

- The bronchoscope is inserted through the nose, and from there passed down the windpipe and into the large airways of the lungs.

- During the procedure, samples of tissue called biopsies may be taken, or fluid may be injected down the tube and sucked out in order to obtain 'washings' from the lungs. These biopsies and washings are then examined in the laboratory.

- After bronchoscopy, you must not eat or drink for 4–6 hours until the local anaesthetic has worn off to prevent the risk of choking.

- If a tissue sample has been taken, you may cough up a small amount of blood over the next few days, but this is quite normal.

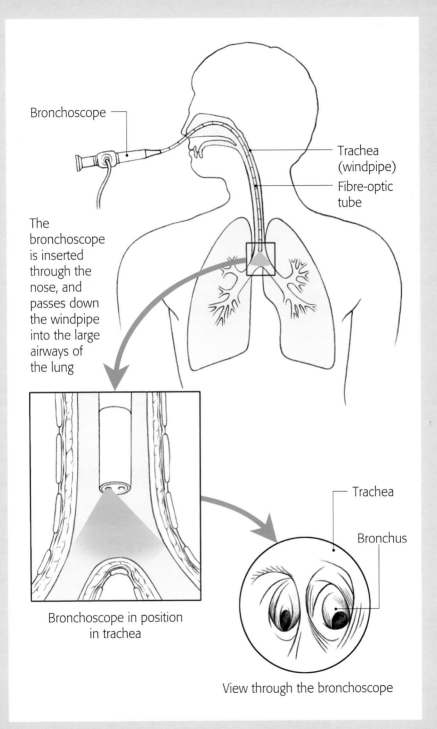

Bronchoscope

Trachea (windpipe)

Fibre-optic tube

The bronchoscope is inserted through the nose, and passes down the windpipe into the large airways of the lung

Bronchoscope in position in trachea

Trachea

Bronchus

View through the bronchoscope

Lung biopsy

- A lung biopsy is necessary when a sample of tissue is needed from an area of lung that cannot be reached using a flexible fibre-optic 'telescope' (bronchoscope). It is usually performed as a day-case procedure.

- A local anaesthetic is injected into the skin over the ribs. The sample of the lung tissue is then taken by inserting a long, thin needle between the ribs. It may be necessary to do this under the guidance of X-rays or a CT scan to pinpoint the area to be sampled.

- If a larger amount of tissue is needed, an 'open' biopsy will be performed under a general anaesthetic.

- An open biopsy involves making a cut up to 15 cm long in the chest to expose the lung so that the sample can be taken. During the operation, a tube is inserted into the chest to allow the lung to expand and will be removed after 1–2 days.

- The average hospital stay following an open biopsy is 2 days.

NEEDLE BIOPSY

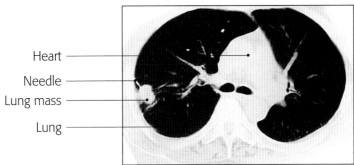

Fine needle
inserted
between ribs

Heart

Needle

Lung mass

Lung

CT scan showing position of biopsy needle

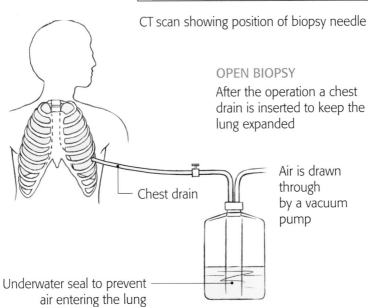

OPEN BIOPSY

After the operation a chest
drain is inserted to keep the
lung expanded

Chest drain

Air is drawn
through
by a vacuum
pump

Underwater seal to prevent
air entering the lung

Asthma – symptoms

- Asthma is difficulty in breathing due to narrowing of the airways.

- Asthma is a very common condition that affects about 10% of children and 5% of adults. It is becoming more common, but the reasons for this are unknown. Asthma may start at any age.

- Asthma is caused by inflammation of the lining of the airways, usually due to an allergic reaction. Inflammation causes the airways to narrow excessively, resulting in wheezing and shortness of breath. In patients with asthma, the airway wall is thicker than normal, and the muscle in the airway is 'twitchy' and liable to go into spasm. The inflammation also irritates the nerves in the airways causing coughing and chest tightness.

- The symptoms of asthma typically vary during the day and may be triggered by various factors. Common triggers for asthma symptoms are exercise, exposure to cold air, laughter, strong smells, breathing in grass pollens or house dust, exposure to pets such as cats, dogs and horses, emotional stress and, in some patients, aspirin and other medicines given for arthritis.

- Asthma is also typically worse at night and may cause awakening in the early hours of the morning. The most severe symptoms may be brought on by a viral infection, such as the common cold.

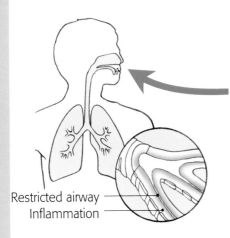

COMMON TRIGGERS FOR ASTHMA
- Exercise
- Cold air
- Laughter
- Strong smells
- Breathing grass pollen
- Emotional stress
- Exposure to pets
- Medicines

Restricted airway
Inflammation

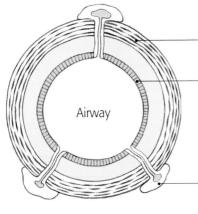

NORMAL AIRWAY

Airway wall made of muscle

Cells lining airway

Airway

Mucous gland

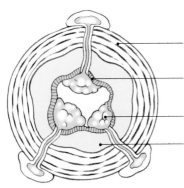

AIRWAY IN ASTHMA

Airway wall muscle thicker than usual and in spasm

The cells lining the airway are often damaged

Mucus production is increased

Inflammatory cells and swelling in airway wall

Asthma – diagnosis

- Asthma is usually diagnosed from the typical symptoms, the type of things that trigger it and the fact that symptoms are relieved with bronchodilator (reliever) drugs.

- The diagnosis may be confirmed by tests of lung function – peak flow measurements and spirometry – which show a narrowing of the airways that can be improved by inhaling a bronchodilator (reliever).

- The peak flow measurement is a convenient measure of how much the airways are narrowed in asthma. Patients blow into a peak flow meter which records the maximum rate at which air can be breathed out. It is also a good indicator of how well asthma is being controlled by treatment – the larger the peak flow measurement, the better the asthma is being controlled.

- Spirometry assesses how well the lungs can work using an instrument called a spirometer.

- Spirometry involves taking a full breath in and then blowing the air out as fast as possible until the lungs are empty. The amount of air breathed out over a period of time is recorded either on a paper chart or electronically.

- Sometimes more complicated lung function tests, such as histamine and exercise tests, are needed to confirm the diagnosis.

- The histamine test is performed in a laboratory. It involves breathing in a spray of histamine of increasing strength until it causes wheezing and this dose is then recorded.

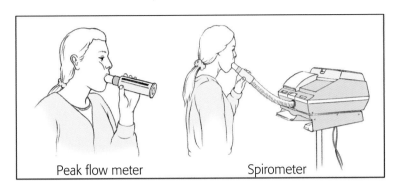

Peak flow meter   Spirometer

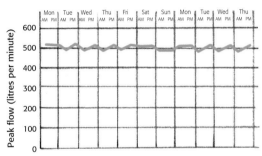

NORMAL PEAK FLOW

Peak flow commonly varies throughout the day and the lowest values are recorded first thing in the morning

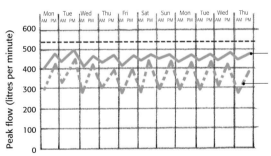

PEAK FLOW IN ASTHMA

— After treatment with reliever inhaler

— Before treatment with reliever inhaler

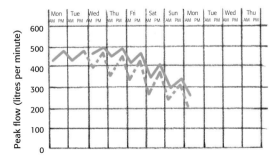

PEAK FLOW IN AN ASTHMA ATTACK

Typically, as an asthma attack develops, the peak flow drops and the response to the reliever is lost. Admission to hospital for treatment is then necessary

Treatment of asthma – relief of symptoms

- Treatment for asthma can be divided into relief of the symptoms and the control of the inflammation of the airways. Drugs which provide relief from the symptoms are commonly called 'relievers' (often coloured blue) and drugs which control the inflammation are called 'preventers' (often coloured brown, maroon or orange).

- 'Relievers' are bronchodilators, which literally means that they open the airways. They do this by relaxing the muscle of the airways to reduce the narrowing and relieve the symptoms.

- The most effective 'relievers' are called beta-agonists. Beta-agonists are best given by inhaler, as this provides rapid relief of symptoms and has fewer side-effects than tablets.

- Short-acting beta-agonists can be used as often as needed to relieve symptoms and their effects last for about 4–6 hours.

- Long-acting beta-agonists are used twice a day to provide longer lasting relief when 'preventers' are not completely effective.

- Other 'relievers' include anticholinergic drugs, such as ipratropium, which is given as an inhaler in addition to a beta-agonist, and theophylline tablets. These drugs are usually used only when asthma is not adequately controlled with beta-agonists and 'preventers'.

- Treatment is varied according to how well the asthma is controlled. This may be monitored by the severity of the symptoms, by the number of times that the reliever inhaler is needed and by measurement of peak flow at home.

Before bronchodilator

After bronchodilator

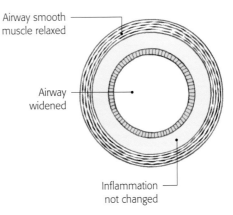

Airway narrowed

Airway smooth muscle relaxed

Airway widened

Tightening of the muscles in the airway

Inflammation not changed

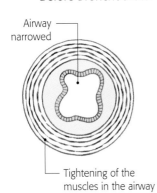

Type of drug	Examples	Trade names
Short-acting beta-agonists	Salbutamol	Ventolin® Salbulin® Airomir®
	Terbutaline Fenoterol	Bricanyl® Berotec®
Long-acting beta-agonists	Salmeterol Formoterol	Serevent® Foradil®
Anticholinergics	Ipratropium Theophylline	Atrovent®
Anticholinergic plus beta-agonist	Ipratropium plus salbutamol Ipratropium plus fenoterol	Combivent® Duovent®

Patients may be given an action plan, often as an individualized 'credit card'. This action plan provides advice about how to increase treatment if the asthma gets worse

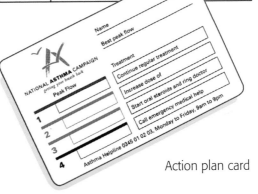

Action plan card

Treatment of asthma – control of inflammation

- Treatment for asthma can be divided into relief of the symptoms and the control of the inflammation of the airways. Drugs which provide relief from the symptoms are commonly called 'relievers' and drugs which control the inflammation are called 'preventers'.

- The most effective 'preventers' are inhaled steroids. These drugs have to be taken on a regular basis, usually twice a day. At the doses needed by most patients with asthma, there are rarely serious side-effects as there are with steroid tablets. The dose is adjusted to give the best control of asthma and it is usually possible to reduce the dose once this has been achieved.

- Other 'preventer' drugs are cromoglycate and nedocromil. These drugs are not as effective as inhaled steroids, but may be useful in mild asthma, particularly in children. They need to be taken four times a day by inhaler.

- Some patients with asthma that is difficult to control will also require theophylline tablets and, occasionally, steroid tablets (usually prednisolone).

Before bronchodilator

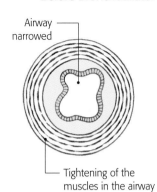

Airway
narrowed

Tightening of the
muscles in the airway

After steroids

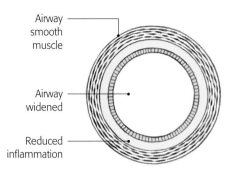

Airway
smooth
muscle

Airway
widened

Reduced
inflammation

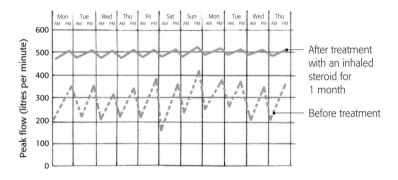

Peak flow (litres per minute)

After treatment
with an inhaled
steroid for
1 month

Before treatment

![inhaler] Type of drug	Examples	Trade names
Inhaled steroids	Beclomethasone dipropionate	Becotide® (low strength) Becloforte® (high strength) Beclazone®
	Budesonide Fluticasone propionate	Pulmicort® Flixotide®
Cromones	Cromoglycate Nedocromil	Intal® Tilade®
Oral steroids	Prednisolone Prednisone Dexamethasone	

Allergen avoidance in asthma

- Allergens trigger an allergic reaction which leads to inflammation and narrowing of the airways. Therefore, an important part of asthma treatment is to reduce exposure to allergens, particularly those which have been shown to make the asthma symptoms worse.

- The most common allergen causing asthma to worsen is the house dust mite. This is found throughout the year and most exposure occurs in the bedroom.

- Domestic pets may also be important in increasing asthma symptoms. Cats are the worst offenders and should be found new homes if possible. On no account should a cat be allowed to sleep on the bed of someone with asthma.

- It is difficult to avoid exposure to grass pollens completely, but bedroom windows should be kept shut during the pollen season (May–July). It is, however, impossible to avoid exposure to mould spores and peak levels are usually seen in late summer and autumn.

- None of these avoidance measures is usually completely successful and medical treatment will also probably be needed.

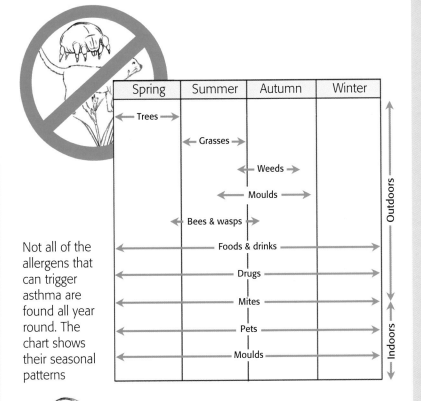

	Spring	Summer	Autumn	Winter
Trees	←→			
Grasses		←→		
Weeds			←→	
Moulds		←——→		
Bees & wasps		←→		
Foods & drinks	←————————————→			
Drugs	←————————————→			
Mites	←————————————→			
Pets	←————————————→			
Moulds	←————————————→			

Outdoors / Indoors

Not all of the allergens that can trigger asthma are found all year round. The chart shows their seasonal patterns

REDUCING EXPOSURE TO HOUSE DUST MITE

- Use special covers for the mattress and pillows (for example, made from Goretex®) that the dust mite cannot penetrate. These are relatively expensive and can be obtained from many chemists

- Use duvets and pillows with synthetic fillings, such as Terylene

- Vacuum and damp dust the bedroom frequently. (Normal vacuum cleaners are as effective as the special vacuum cleaners sold to reduce house dust mite)

- Replace carpets with vinyl floor coverings and curtains with blinds

- Remove all soft furnishings from the bedroom

Acute asthma attacks

- Asthma attacks may occur at any time. An attack may come 'out of the blue', or may be triggered by a virus infection such as the common cold or 'flu, by exposure to a large dose of allergens (for example, in the grass pollen season) or by stopping treatment with 'preventer' drugs.

- Asthma symptoms usually get worse gradually, with an increase in symptoms and more frequent use of 'reliever' drugs (beta-agonists). Often the beta-agonist does not work as well or last as long as it did previously.

- The severity of the asthma attack will be reflected in your peak flow measurements and your personal action plan should be followed.

- A severe attack of asthma can make you so breathless that it is difficult to talk or eat. If your asthma is this severe, you will have to go to hospital immediately for emergency treatment.

- After an attack, the response to treatment is monitored by peak flow measurements. It is often necessary to repeat the nebulizer treatment until the peak flow reaches a satisfactory level.

- Once the attack is under control, the steroid tablets must be continued until the peak flow returns to normal (usually 1–2 weeks). It is important to monitor your peak flow at home after leaving hospital to make sure recovery continues; sometimes, it may be necessary to increase the steroid dose again.

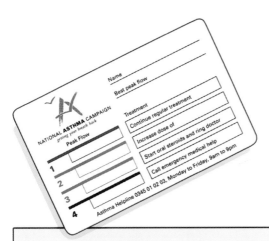

TREATMENT OF A SEVERE ASTHMA ATTACK

Treatment of a severe attack may be started by your GP, in the ambulance or in the casualty department

- Oxygen is given through a face mask, as the level of oxygen in the blood falls when the attack is severe

- A beta-agonist is given by nebulizer or sometimes by inhaler (20 puffs) through a large volume spacer to open the airways. (An anti-cholinergic may be added to the beta-agonist if the initial response is not satisfactory)

- Steroid tablets are given as soon as possible. Initially, the steroids may be given by injection and then switched to tablets

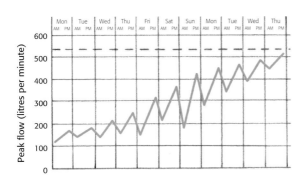

The peak flow is monitored and rises as the asthma gets better

Chronic bronchitis

- Chronic bronchitis is inflammation of the airways that is usually caused by irritants in tobacco smoke. The irritation stimulates the airways to produce increased amounts of sputum (mucus or phlegm). This occurs for more than 3 months of the year and is usually worse in winter.

- Some patients with chronic bronchitis also have asthma.

- The most effective treatment for chronic bronchitis is to stop smoking. After stopping smoking, the amount of sputum that is produced will gradually decrease over several months.

- Chest infections are more common in people with chronic bronchitis. These infections are associated with a change in the colour of the sputum from white or grey to yellow or green, and there may be flecks of blood. There may also be shortness of breath and wheezing.

- Chest infections need antibiotic treatment, which should usually be taken for 1–2 weeks.

- Patients with chronic bronchitis may be advised to be vaccinated against 'flu (influenza). This is because 'flu may also lead to chest infections.

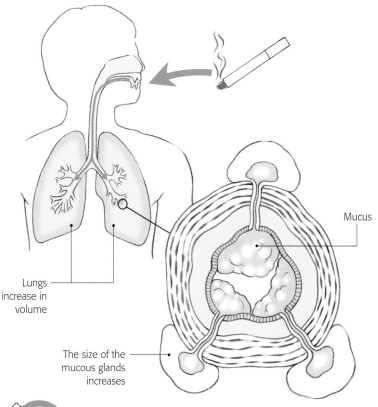

Mucus

Lungs
increase in
volume

The size of the
mucous glands
increases

TIPS TO STOP SMOKING

- Nicotine in the form of chewing gum (Nicorette®) or skin patches (Nicorette®, Nicabate®, Niconil®, Nicotinel®) may help you to stop smoking, though the patches are more effective. Both are available on prescription

- There are special clinics devoted to helping people to stop smoking and there are special telephone help lines that can be very supportive

- Hypnosis may sometimes be helpful

Bronchiectasis

- Bronchiectasis is a long-standing infection of the airways of the lung. It is usually the result of a previous severe chest infection, but may also be seen in cystic fibrosis.

- Bronchiectasis results in persistent coughing and the continuous production of yellow or green sputum (mucus or phlegm), which may get worse from time to time when the infection increases.

- Treatment for bronchiectasis usually consists of constant daily antibiotics and physiotherapy to help drain the sputum from the lungs. Sometimes antibiotics are given only when there is an increase in the amount of sputum produced. This is because constant treatment may lead to infection with bacteria that are not readily treated with antibiotics.

- Physiotherapy involves positioning yourself so that the sputum can be coughed up from the lungs more easily. You will be given an appointment with a physiotherapist who will teach you how to do this.

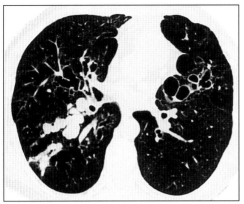

CT scan showing
the widened
airways in
bronchiectasis

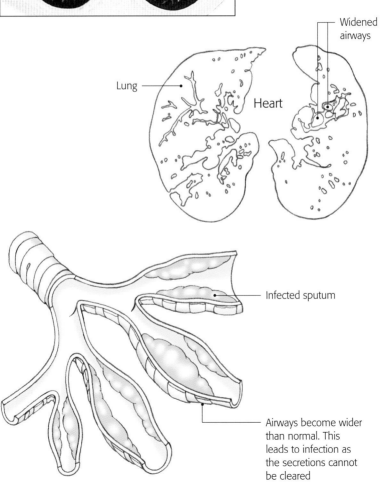

Widened
airways

Lung

Heart

Infected sputum

Airways become wider
than normal. This
leads to infection as
the secretions cannot
be cleared

Chronic obstructive pulmonary disease and emphysema

● Chronic obstructive pulmonary disease (COPD) is the name given to the progressive narrowing of the airways that develops in some patients who smoke. This narrowing may result from an obstruction of the airways in patients with chronic bronchitis (as a result of scarring of the airway and sputum secretion) or emphysema.

● Emphysema is brought about by cigarette smoking which results in chemical changes that destroy lung tissue. The loss of lung tissue means that the elastic effect of the lung surrounding the small airways is reduced, so that the airways tend to close more easily. The alveoli become damaged and the area of lung that is available for gas exchange is reduced.

● The symptoms of COPD are progressive shortness of breath on exercise and eventually breathlessness even at rest. Symptoms slowly get worse over a number of years, but may get worse after a chest infection.

● Patients with COPD caused by chronic bronchitis may also have a cough and bring up increased amounts of sputum (mucus or phlegm). When the condition is severe, there may be ankle swelling caused by the strain put on the heart.

● The only treatment that has been shown to reverse the progression of COPD is to give up smoking. However, the symptoms can be relieved by bronchodilator ('reliever') drugs which are given by inhaler or nebulizer.

● Acute attacks are often the result of a chest infection and are usually treated with antibiotics.

CHRONIC BRONCHITIS

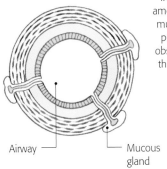

Airway — — Mucous gland

Normal airway

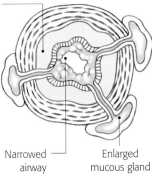

Increased amounts of mucus are produced obstructing the airway

Narrowed airway — — Enlarged mucous gland

Airway in chronic bronchitis

EMPHYSEMA

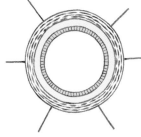

Normally, the airway is held open by elastic lung attachments ('guy ropes')

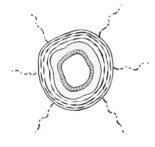

Lung attachments are broken down in emphysema, closing off the airways

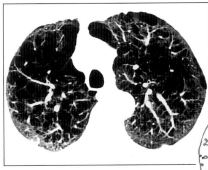

CT scan showing the widespread destruction of lung tissue, creating big 'holes'

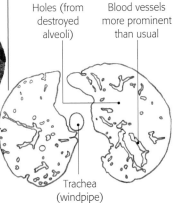

Holes (from destroyed alveoli)   Blood vessels more prominent than usual

Trachea (windpipe)

Chest infections and pneumonia

- Acute tracheitis is caused by an infection of the windpipe (trachea). This causes a painful cough and a pain behind the breastbone. It is usually caused by a viral infection, and there is no specific treatment apart from painkillers and cough medicines. Antibiotics are usually unnecessary unless the sputum (mucus or phlegm) is yellow.

- Acute bronchitis is caused by an infection of the airways. It may develop after a virus infection and is more common in smokers. Antibiotics are usually unnecessary unless the sputum (mucus or phlegm) is yellow.

- Pneumonia is an infection of the lung itself. It shows up on a chest X-ray as a white patch, which may be confined to one lobe of the lung (lobar pneumonia) or may be patchily spread throughout the lungs (bronchopneumonia).

- Pneumonia may cause shortness of breath, cough and production of yellow or green sputum. There may be pain due to pleurisy, which is inflammation of the membrane lining the lungs. Other signs of infection, such as a high temperature, sweating, loss of appetite, tiredness and a feeling of illness, are also usually present.

- Treatment for pneumonia consists of antibiotics and fluids. If the pneumonia is severe or due to an unusual infection, you will need to be admitted to hospital, where the antibiotics and fluids may be given through a 'drip' directly into the veins.

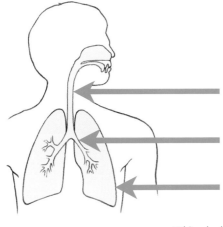

Acute tracheitis – infection of the windpipe

Acute bronchitis – infection of the airways

Pneumonia – infection of the lungs

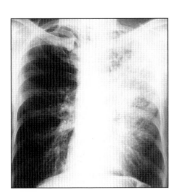

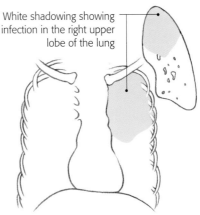

White shadowing showing infection in the right upper lobe of the lung

Lobar pneumonia

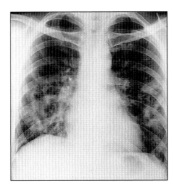

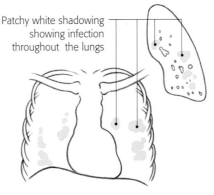

Patchy white shadowing showing infection throughout the lungs

Patchy bronchopneumonia

Tuberculosis

- Tuberculosis is caused by infection with a bacterium called *Mycobacterium tuberculosis*. Tuberculosis develops slowly and, as a result, is often diagnosed late.
- The lungs are the most common site of infection. Symptoms usually include a dry cough, sometimes with small amounts of sputum (mucus or phlegm) that may be tinged with blood. There may also be weight loss, a slight fever, and a general feeling of weakness and tiredness.
- The chest X-ray may show a typical shadow with a cavity, often in the upper part of the lungs. The bacteria responsible for tuberculosis may be seen in a sputum sample using a microscope, but usually have to be grown in the laboratory for 8 weeks before they can be detected.
- A skin test (the Mantoux test) may be performed if the diagnosis is uncertain. The test involves injecting an extract of tuberculosis bacteria into the skin. A positive test results in redness and swelling of the skin 24 hours later.
- Tuberculosis is treated with special drugs and at least three drugs are used at the same time in order to prevent the bacteria becoming resistant to treatment. It is important that the drugs are taken regularly and this may be supervised by health visitors in the chest clinic.
- Because tuberculosis is infectious, it is important to trace contacts and to examine close contacts for any signs of the disease. This is done by taking a chest X-ray and carrying out a skin test.

SITES AND SYMPTOMS

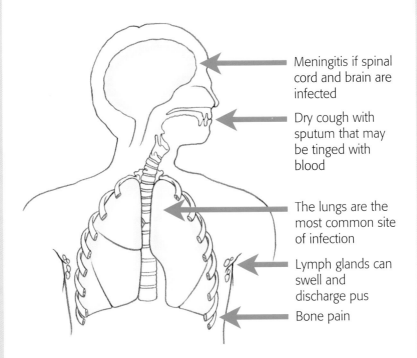

Meningitis if spinal cord and brain are infected

Dry cough with sputum that may be tinged with blood

The lungs are the most common site of infection

Lymph glands can swell and discharge pus

Bone pain

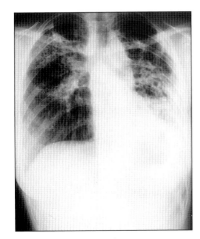

Chest X-ray showing widespread tuberculosis

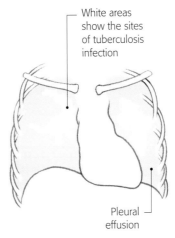

White areas show the sites of tuberculosis infection

Pleural effusion

Pleurisy and pleural effusion

- Pleurisy is inflammation of the pleural membranes lining the lungs. It is usually caused by pneumonia, but may occur as a result of a blood clot in the lung (pulmonary embolism) or on its own.

- Pleurisy causes a severe sharp pain in the chest, which is made worse by breathing in and by coughing. The pain is typically sharp and can usually be pinpointed to a particular spot in the chest.

- A pleural effusion is a collection of fluid in the space between the pleural membranes. It may occur as a result of pleurisy overlying an area of pneumonia. Sometimes it develops slowly and the only symptom may be shortness of breath as the fluid accumulates to such an extent that it compresses the lung underneath.

- It may be necessary to obtain a sample of pleural fluid to find the underlying cause or to remove the fluid to make breathing easier.

- A local anaesthetic is injected into the skin and a needle inserted between the ribs into the pleural space. The fluid is then drawn off into the syringe. Sometimes more than 1 litre of fluid can be removed. The procedure can be repeated if more fluid accumulates.

- Sometimes pleural effusions become infected and the pleural fluid becomes like pus. This is called empyema. This is treated with strong antibiotics and frequent drainage of the fluid. If the fluid collects in 'pockets', it can be difficult to drain and an operation is necessary to remove it.

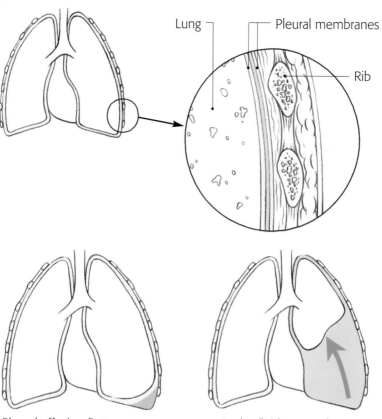

20

Lung

Pleural membranes

Rib

Pleural effusion first appears as a collection of fluid in a corner of the lungs

As the fluid accumulates, it compresses the lung

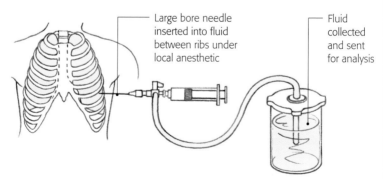

Large bore needle inserted into fluid between ribs under local anesthetic

Fluid collected and sent for analysis

Fluid may be collected to find the underlying cause or to make breathing easier

Pneumothorax

- Pneumothorax is the collapse of a lung, usually as a result of a small leak developing on the lung surface. This allows air into the pleural space.

- The most common type of pneumothorax occurs without warning after trauma (e.g. a road traffic accident), but it can also occur as a complication of other lung diseases, such as tuberculosis, certain types of pneumonia and occasionally a severe asthma attack.

- The symptoms of pneumothorax usually include shortness of breath due to the lung collapse and often chest pain.

- Treatment involves putting in a chest drain to draw out the air. A local anaesthetic is injected into the overlying skin and a sharp probe inserted into the pleural space. A drainage tube is then passed into the pleural space and suction applied for several days until the lung expands fully – this is checked on a chest X-ray.

- If pneumothorax occurs repeatedly, an operation may be necessary. This involves removing the pleural space by roughening the pleural membrane with irritants so that the lung 'sticks' to the chest wall and cannot collapse.

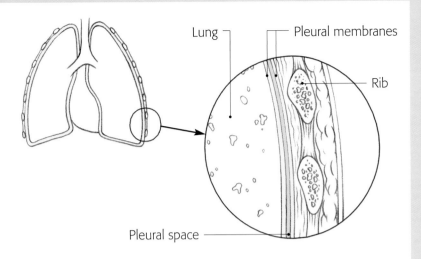

21

Lung
Pleural membranes
Rib
Pleural space

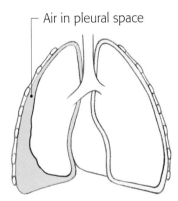

Air in pleural space

Small pneumothorax

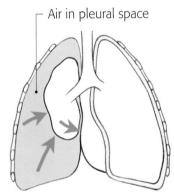

Air in pleural space

Large pneumothorax causing
the lung to collapse and
pushing the heart and other
lung away

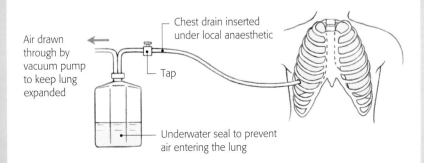

Chest drain inserted
under local anaesthetic

Air drawn
through by
vacuum pump
to keep lung
expanded

Tap

Underwater seal to prevent
air entering the lung

Pulmonary embolism

- A pulmonary embolism occurs when clots of blood, which may form anywhere in the body, but most commonly in the deep veins of legs, are carried in the blood to the lungs where they become lodged.

- Blood clots are more likely to occur during periods of prolonged immobility, for example during illness. The blood may also be more likely to clot in some diseases and in some women taking the contraceptive pill.

- Clots which reach the lung may block the circulation and damage the lung. This may lead to inflammation of the lining of the lung (pleurisy) which causes a sharp chest pain, and may cause blood to be coughed up.

- Repeated clots or large clots increase the damage to the lung, and may eventually affect the circulation and put a strain on the heart.

- Pulmonary embolism is treated with anticoagulants which thin the blood. These will usually be given initially as injections of heparin and followed by tablets of warfarin. Regular blood tests are necessary when these drugs are being taken to ensure that the correct dose is being given.

- People who are considered to have a high risk of developing clots may be given anticoagulants as a preventative treatment. This is usually only given before an operation, but patients who have had several blood clots may need to continue to take anticoagulants for a longer period of time.

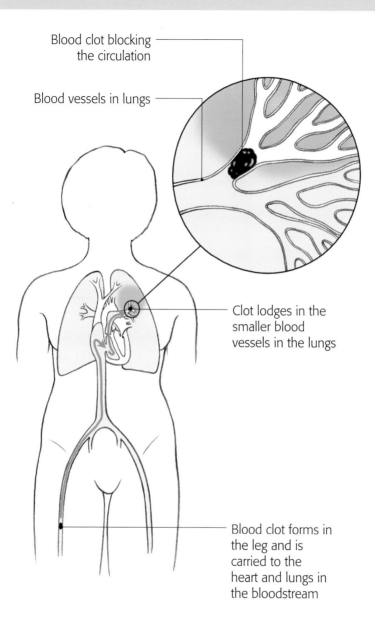

Blood clot blocking the circulation

Blood vessels in lungs

Clot lodges in the smaller blood vessels in the lungs

Blood clot forms in the leg and is carried to the heart and lungs in the bloodstream

Lung tumours and cancer

- A lung tumour is any growth in the lung. Lung tumours usually appear as a solid shadow on the chest X-ray.

- Benign tumours are non-cancerous growths, which usually enlarge slowly. They are usually removed by surgery because they may block the airways.

- Malignant tumours or cancers grow steadily and may spread to other parts of the lung and outside the lung through the blood. The most common lung cancers are linked to cigarette smoking.

- Sometimes malignant tumours in the lung arise from cancers that have spread from other parts of the body, such as the gut, breast or prostate gland.

- Lung cancer may cause symptoms in the lung, such as chest pain, coughing and coughing up blood, as well as more general symptoms, such as weight loss and a feeling of being unwell.

- Spread of the cancer outside the lung may lead to other symptoms, such as pain in the bones or swelling of the liver which causes discomfort and pain.

- Although lung cancer may be likely from the appearance of the chest X-ray, it is usually necessary to obtain a tissue sample by bronchoscopy or lung biopsy. The tumour can then be examined using a microscope in order to determine the type of cancer, which is important when deciding on treatment.

- Other imaging investigations may be performed to assess the size of the cancer and whether it has spread to lymph glands in the lung or outside the lung to the liver and bones.

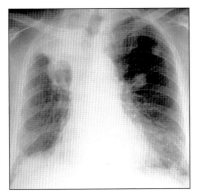

Chest X-ray showing
widespread lung cancer

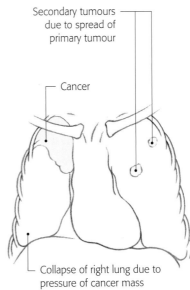

Secondary tumours
due to spread of
primary tumour

Cancer

Collapse of right lung due to
pressure of cancer mass

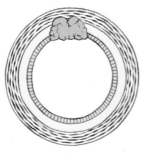

Cancer cells start to grow

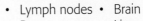

- Lymph nodes   • Brain
- Bones   • Liver

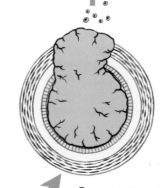

Cancer may spread
(develop secondaries)

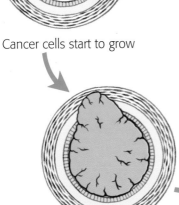

Cancer may block off an airway

Treatment of lung cancer

- The treatment given for lung cancer will depend on the type of cancer and whether it has spread.

- If the cancer is very small and has not spread, it may be possible to remove the affected part of the lung in an operation.

- The main treatments for cancer that has spread are radiotherapy and chemotherapy. These treatments may be combined.

- Radiotherapy involves directing a beam of X-rays into the affected lung to reduce the size of the tumour. Radiotherapy is also used to treat cancer that has spread to other sites, such as the bones. Treatment is usually given once a week over several weeks on an out-patient basis. Unfortunately, it may cause side-effects, such as nausea and vomiting.

- Chemotherapy usually involves giving injections of a 'cocktail' of anti-cancer drugs over a period of several weeks. This will often shrink the tumour at the original site and at any sites to which it has spread. Patients may be treated as out-patients or may be admitted to hospital overnight.

- Unfortunately, chemotherapy often has unpleasant side-effects, such as nausea and vomiting, that will need special treatment. Hair loss is also common.

- Other treatments that may be necessary include strong painkillers, such as morphine, and drugs to stop the nausea brought on by chemotherapy and radiotherapy.

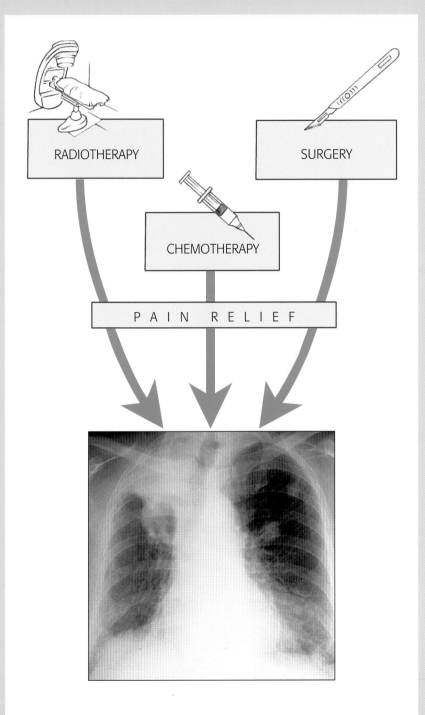

Cystic fibrosis

- Cystic fibrosis is the most common inherited disease. It affects 1 out of every 2000 people born in the UK. Cystic fibrosis usually appears in childhood, but is occasionally diagnosed in adults.

- Cystic fibrosis is caused by a fault in the gene that controls the secretions in epithelial cells lining the airways, the gut and the pancreas. It results in abnormally thick secretions in the airways and poor absorption of food from the gut.

- Chronic infection of the lungs (bronchiectasis) is one of the most common features of cystic fibrosis. Copious amounts of very sticky, yellow/green sputum (mucus or phlegm) are produced. This makes breathing progressively more difficult.

- The poor absorption of food is caused by the failure of the pancreas to secrete substances which are necessary for digestion. This may result in malnutrition. Some patients also develop diabetes.

- Tests for cystic fibrosis include a chest X-ray and a sweat test. In some specialist centres, the disease can also now be diagnosed by a blood test that can detect the genetic defect in DNA.

- The sweat test involves causing the skin to sweat using a weak electrical current, but this will not cause any discomfort. The sweat is then collected and the salt content analysed. In patients with cystic fibrosis the salt content is higher than in other people.

- The disease usually slowly gets worse, although the outlook is much better with modern antibiotic treatment.

Sticky sputum is produced
which leads to chronic
infection of the lungs –
bronchiectasis

Poor absorption of food
caused by failure of the
pancreas to secrete substances
necessary for digestion

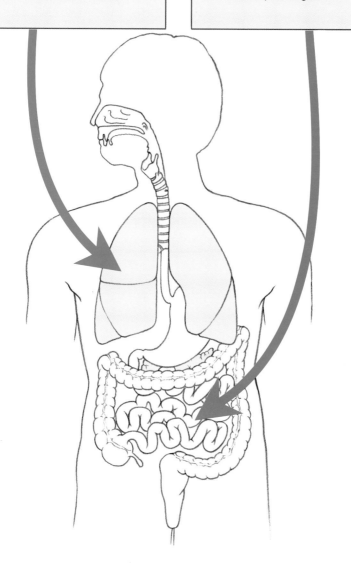

Treatment of cystic fibrosis

- Treatment for cystic fibrosis aims to control the lung infections and improve the digestion of food.

- Antibiotics that are effective against the bacteria that most commonly cause lung infections may be given as tablets or by nebulizer when the infection is severe.

- DNAse (Pulmozyme®) given by nebulizer may be useful in some patients to reduce the stickiness and viscosity of the sputum. It is usually given for a trial period of 4 weeks as it is not effective in all patients.

- Physiotherapy is also very important to help clear the sticky secretions from the lung.

- A pancreatic enzyme supplement, which should be taken before meals, is given to improve the absorption of food. Vitamin supplements are also often given.

- Lung transplantation offers the best hope when the disease becomes very severe, and the outlook after transplantation is good.

- Research into other forms of therapy involving the manipulation of genes is being carried out, but it is likely to be a long time before this type of treatment will be useful.

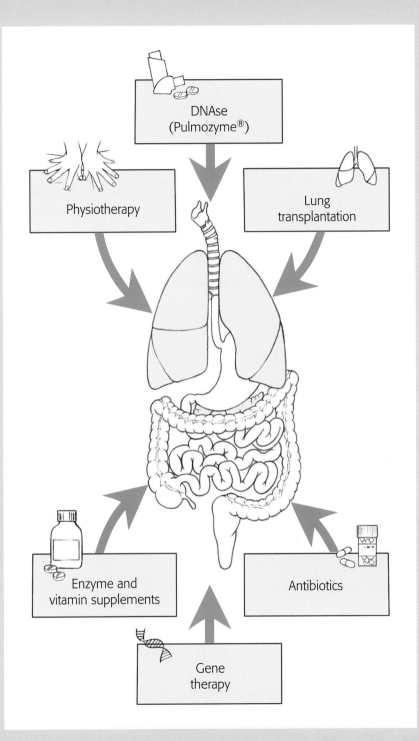

Inhaler devices

- Inhalers are the best way to administer treatment in asthma and chronic obstructive pulmonary disease, as they deliver the drug directly to the lungs and this reduces side-effects. It is important, however, that the inhaler is used correctly.

- An automatic metered dose inhaler is available to help those patients who find it difficult to coordinate breathing in with timing the activation of the device. The automatic inhaler is used in the same way as a manual inhaler, but the dose is fired off automatically on breathing in (a click is heard as the device triggers).

- Large volume spacers are often used in combination with a manual metered dose inhaler. The large volume spacer acts as a reservoir for the cloud of drug produced by the inhaler. Use of the spacer delivers a larger amount of drug to the lungs and reduces the amount of drug deposited in the mouth. This is particularly important when steroids are being given.

- When a large volume spacer is being used, the inhaler is activated in the same way as usual. Only one dose should be used at a time. Spacer devices can be fitted with a face mask, so that they can be used to treat even small children.

- Dry powder inhalers are becoming more popular as they are convenient and easier to use than metered dose inhalers.

27

Inhaler

Inhaler with large volume spacer

Dry powder inhaler

Spacer with face mask

HOW TO USE AN INHALER CORRECTLY

- Remove the cap and shake the inhaler

- Breathe out gently

- Place the mouthpiece in your mouth, then breathe in slowly while activating the device (by pressing the canister down)

- Continue to breathe in until your lungs are full

- Hold your breath for a count of 10 to allow the spray to reach the deeper parts of the lung

- Only one dose at a time should be used

Home nebulizers

- Nebulizers are useful in treating severe asthma attacks in children and in patients with very severe airway obstruction who find it difficult to use an inhaler.

- Nebulizers are also useful for giving antibiotics to patients with cystic fibrosis, and to treat and prevent pneumonia due to a bacterium called *Pneumocystis carinii* in patients with AIDS.

- There are two types of nebulizer that can be used at home. One type uses an electrical compressor and the other type uses ultrasonic vibration.

- Several drugs are available for use in nebulizers. These may come in the form of a solution that has to be measured out with a syringe, or in already measured single-dose units.

- To use the nebulizer, it should first be plugged in. The drug solution should then be poured into the nebulizer chamber and the chamber closed. The machine is then switched on. The mist that is generated should then be breathed in normally through the mouthpiece or face mask. When all of the drug has been used, the nebulizer will 'splutter' (this normally takes about 10 minutes and there is often a small amount of liquid left).

- It is important to look after the nebulizer. The mouthpiece or face mask should be washed in warm water, and the nebulizer should be dried out after use.

28

Compressor nebulizer

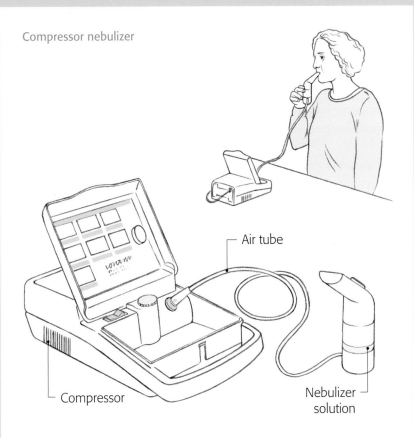

Air tube

Compressor

Nebulizer solution

ULTRASONIC NEBULIZER

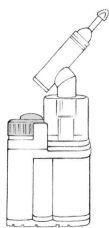

Nebulizers produce a fine mist which can then be inhaled, either through a mouthpiece or, in small children, through a face mask

Home oxygen therapy

- Oxygen may be provided at home for some patients with severe lung disease, especially if the condition is putting a strain on the heart. Oxygen can improve the symptoms of breathlessness and make it possible to do more at home.

- Before oxygen is recommended for home use, a careful assessment is usually made. This may involve exercise tests and measurements of blood oxygen levels, both with and without oxygen therapy.

- There are two main ways of providing oxygen at home. The traditional method is with liquid oxygen cylinders, which have to be delivered and are heavy. More recently, oxygen concentrators have been developed that concentrate oxygen from the air. These devices are about the size of a fridge and run off the main electricity supply.

- Home oxygen is not given to patients who still smoke, because of the danger that a cigarette may ignite the oxygen.

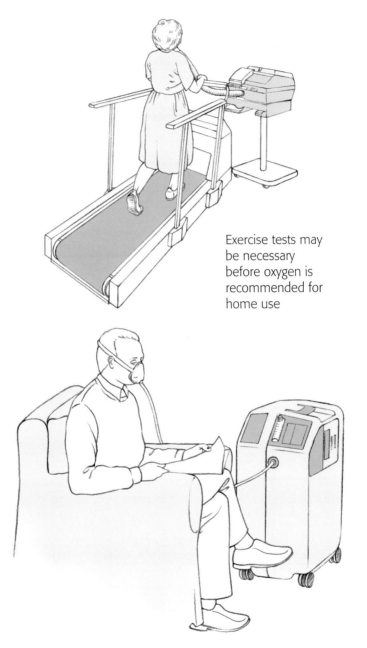

29

Exercise tests may be necessary before oxygen is recommended for home use

Oxygen concentrators concentrate oxygen from the air and avoid the need to have heavy oxygen cylinders delivered to your home

Mail Order

Additional copies of this book and other titles in the *Patient Pictures* series are available at a unit price of £12 (post-paid in the UK only).

Current titles include:
- Cardiology
- Fertility
- Gastroenterology
- Gynaecology
- HIV medicine
- Prostatic diseases and treatments
- Respiratory diseases
- Rheumatology
- Urological surgery

Please order from our website, www.healthpress.co.uk, or to receive a brochure, send your name and address to:

Health Press Limited
Elizabeth House
Queen Street
Abingdon
Oxford OX14 3JR
UK

Health Press titles are available at special discounts when purchased in bulk quantities for trusts, associations or institutions. Please call our Special Sales Department in Abingdon on:

Tel: 01235 523233
Fax: 01235 523238